The Atlas of
DIABOLICAL
DINOSAURS
AND OTHER AMAZING CREATURES OF THE MESOZOIC

First published in the UK in 2021
by NQ Publishers, an imprint
of Nextquisite Ltd, 105 Grand Parade,
Leigh-On-Sea SS9 1DW, England.
www.nextquisite.com.
Copyright © 2021 Nextquisite Ltd

Project Director Anne McRae
Illustrations Daniel Hamilton
Design Marco Nardi
Text Dora Martin
Editing Susan Bishop

ISBN 978-1-912944-37-8

Printed in Slovakia

The Atlas of
DIABOLICAL
DINOSAURS

AND OTHER AMAZING CREATURES OF THE MESOZOIC

Written by Dora Martin – Illustrated by Daniel Hamilton

NQ
PUBLISHERS
For enquiring minds

TABLE OF CONTENTS

A WORLD OF DINOSAURS

We are living through a golden age of dinosaur discovery. A new generation of palaeontologists is using traditional fieldwork and the latest technology to uncover about 50 entirely new species every year — that's almost one a week!

The dinosaur with the longest name is Micropachycephalosaurus. It means "tiny, thick-headed lizard."

Ophthalmosaurus
165–160 MYA

Leptoceratops
67–66 MYA

Plateosaurus
214–204 MYA

Tyrannosaurus rex
68–66 MYA

Pachycephalosaurus
76–66 MYA

Torvosaurus
153–148 MYA

Spinosaurus
99–75 MYA

Anabisetia
93–89 MYA

Amargasaurus
129–122 MYA

Riojasaurus
228–208 MYA

Stegosaurus
155–145 MYA

Stegosaurus is the largest and best known member of the stegosaur family. Stegosaurs lived in large herds, feasting on low-lying plants and fallen fruit.

Austroraptor
85–66 MYA

The discovery of feathered dinosaurs in China in the 1990s changed the way we think about dinosaurs and made it clear, for the first time, that modern birds are the direct descendants of dinosaurs.

Mamenchisaurus
160–145 MYA

Plant-eating sauropods were the largest dinosaurs ever to walk the Earth. With their lengthy necks and tails, some were almost as long as two articulated lorries.

Balaur
72–66 MYA

Microraptor
135–113 MYA

The biggest pterosaurs were about the same size as a modern light aircraft.

Giant Mongolian pterosaur
About 70 MYA

Struthiosaurus
83–66 MYA

Therizinosaurus
75–70 MYA

Anchiornis
168–151 MYA

Askeptosaurus
247–225 MYA

Gigantspinosaurus
163–157 MYA

Dilong
128–127 MYA

Alwalkeria
237–208 MYA

Isanosaurus
105–93 MYA

Zhenyuanlong
About 125 MYA

Mansourasaurus
About 80 MYA

Plesiosaurus
199–175 MYA

Liopleurodon
166–140 MYA

Giraffatitan
163–145 MYA

Tuatara
From 250 MYA

Eocursor
228–201 MYA

Muttaburrasaurus
105–93 MYA

Antarctanax
About 250 MYA

Cartorhynchus
About 248 MYA

Ceratopsids like Triceratops and Hellboy had wildly elaborate displays of bony horns and frills on their skulls.

Hellboy
About 68 MYA

Many other creatures lived alongside the dinosaurs. Some of their descendants, such as crocodiles and turtles, have survived but others, like the pterosaurs, are gone for ever.

GEOLOGICAL TIME

Planet Earth formed about 4.6 billion years ago. The first living things appeared around four billion years ago but life didn't become abundant until the Cambrian period, about 550 million years ago. The dinosaurs lived during the Mesozoic era, between about 252–66 MYA.

Earth scientists, such as geologists and palaeontologists, divide the Earth's long history into time spans. The longest spans are called eons. They are divided into eras which are in turn divided into periods and epochs.

CENOZOIC	**QUATERNARY**	HOLOCENE	11,700 YEARS AGO
		PLEISTOCENE	1.8 MYA
	TERTIARY	PLIOCENE	5.3 MYA
		MIOCENE	23 MYA
		OLIGOCENE	33.9 MYA
		EOCENE	55.8 MYA
		PALEOCENE	66 MYA

MASS EXTINCTION

MESOZOIC	CRETACEOUS	145.5 MYA
	JURASSIC	199.6 MYA
	TRIASSIC	252 MYA

MASS EXTINCTION

PALEOZOIC	PERMIAN	299 MYA
	CARBONIFEROUS	360 MYA
	DEVONIAN	416 MYA
	SILURIAN	443 MYA
	ORDOVICIAN	488.3 MYA
	CAMBRIAN	542 MYA

PRE-CAMBRIAN	PROTEROZOIC	2.5 BYA
	ARCHEAN	
	HADEAN	

EARTH'S FORMATION

Age of mammals

People

Mammal

Flowering plants

Age of dinosaurs

First birds

First mammals

Dinosaur

Reptiles

Insects

Fishes

Land plants

Spiders

Jawless fish

Trilobites

Charnia

Stromatolites

DISCOVERING DINOSAURS

Dinosaur science officially began in Britain in 1842 when the brilliant but rather snarky naturalist Richard Owen coined the word dinosaur, or "terrible lizard." Scientists had been collecting and describing fossils that turned out to be dinosaurs for 150 years before then, but it was Owen's genius that identified them as a single group of reptiles.

WHAT IS A FOSSIL?

Almost everything we know about dinosaurs and other extinct creatures is based on the study of fossils. A fossil is the remains of a plant or animal that has undergone a preservation process (often lasting thousands or millions of years). Most fossils are the hard parts of an animal, such as bones, that have turned to stone.

Right: How a dinosaur became a fossil that palaeontologists could find.

4. Excavation

Movements in the Earth's crust carry the deeply buried corpse to the surface where chance discovery or targeted searches bring it to the attention of scientists.

3. Fossilisation

Over a very long time, minerals seep into the animal's bones, turning them to stone.

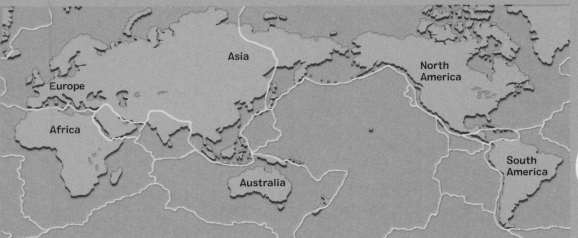

Above: Here you can see the main tectonic plates in the Earth's crust. They are about 100 km (61 mi) thick.

Continents adrift

Each chapter in this book begins with a map of a continent and shows the dinosaurs that lived there. There are also three maps to show you where modern continents were located during each period of the dinosaur age.

LATE TRIASSIC

PANGAEA

When dinosaurs first evolved during the Triassic period, all the continents were united in a single large landmass called Pangaea.

LATE JURASSIC

LAURASIA

GONDWANA

About 200 million years ago, at the start of the Jurassic period, Pangaea began to split into two new continents: Gondwana in the south and Laurasia in the north.

LATE CRETACEOUS

LAURASIA

GONDWANA

By the end of the Cretaceous period, the continents we know today were already recognisable, although they were in very different positions from their current ones.

CONTINENTAL DRIFT

The Earth's crust is broken into seven very large slabs of rock and about a dozen smaller ones. Scientists call these slabs of rock tectonic plates. The plates are constantly on the move, riding like rafts on the softer rock of the Earth's mantle and carrying the continents and islands with them as they drift. The continents we know today are very different to the ones that existed during the dinosaur age.

1. Death

When an animal dies it is usually eaten by scavengers, but some fall into in a river or lake and sink to the bottom.

Palaeontology is the scientific study of life before the Holocene epoch that began about 11,700 years ago.

2. Decomposition

The corpse is gradually covered by mud and sand. The dead animal's flesh slowly rots away.

OH, THE MISTAKES WE MADE!

Dinosaurs are very different to modern animals and early palaeontologists were often baffled by them. As they tried to make sense of the fossils and reconstruct their skeletons they made some hilarious blunders.

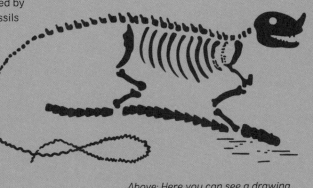

Below: This is a drawing of a Diplodocus from 1916. Its legs are splayed out to the sides like a modern crocodile. It took some time for scientists to agree that the legs should be straight up and down, like an elephant's.

Above: Here you can see a drawing of an Iguanodon's skeleton with its thumb spike stuck onto its snout like a rhinoceros horn! It was only when a whole herd of Iguanodon skeletons was found in Belgium that scientists realised that it belonged on the creatures' thumbs.

THE MESOZOIC ERA

Dinosaurs ruled the Earth for at least 165 million years. They were the dominant land animals for most of the Mesozoic era. At the same time, the seas were teeming with creatures unlike any alive today, such as plesiosaurs and mosasaurs, and the skies were home to strange flying animals we now call pterosaurs. The Mesozoic world was very different to the one we know now.

THE TRIASSIC PERIOD

The Triassic dawned on the heels of the Great Dying, the largest extinction event the world has ever known. More than 90 per cent of all life was wiped out, probably by a mixture of volcanic activity and global warming. As the planet recovered, the few species that had survived slowly repopulated the empty habitats. New creatures appeared, such as small mammals, while some reptiles evolved into the first dinosaurs. The Triassic climate was hot and dry. The Earth's landmasses were all joined in the supercontinent of Pangaea which was surrounded by a vast ocean called Panthalassa. By the end of the Triassic, the seas were filled with life, including giant reptiles like the dolphin-shaped ichthyosaurs and long-necked plesiosaurs.

THE JURASSIC PERIOD

Pangaea had split in two by the beginning of the Jurassic, with Laurasia to the north and Gondwana to the south. As they slowly broke into smaller landmasses, seas flooded in between, making the climate more humid. Plants flourished in the subtropical conditions and new species of giant sauropod dinosaurs like Diplodocus and Mamenchisaurus evolved to feast on them. Other new herbivores included the stegosaurs with their plated spines. As the numbers and types of plant-eating dinosaurs grew, new predators appeared to feed on them, such as the fearsome Allosaurus. Reptiles continued to flourish in the seas, while Archaeopterx — the earliest known bird — took to the skies alongside the pterosaurs.

Kentrosaurus
200 MYA

Mamenchisaurus
163–140 MYA

Citipati *was an oviraptorid dinosaur that lived in Mongolia. Many well preserved skeletons have been found so it is quite well known.*

Hornby Island *lies off the east coast of Canada. It was home to a pterosaur that was about the size of a pet cat.*

Styracosaurus *was a large ceratopsid dinosaur. The spike on its nose could grow up to 60 cm (2 ft) long.*

Siats meekerorum *was a very large predatory dinosaur that lived in North America. Siats was related to the earlier Allosaurus.*

THE CRETACEOUS PERIOD

Dinosaurs were more numerous and varied during the Cretaceous than at any other time. New groups evolved and by the late Cretaceous tyrannosaurs preyed on herds of hadrosaurs, ceratopsids and anklyosaurs in North America and Eurasia, while titanosaurs were hunted by abelisaurs and carcharodontosaurs in the southern continents. There were many primitive birds in the skies. In the seas, the snakelike mosasaurs took over from the plesiosaurs. On land, small mammals flourished. By the end of the period the continents were shaped much as they are today. Some scientists believe that the dinosaurs were already in decline by this time. Then, about 66 million years ago, a catastrophic event brought the Cretaceous, and the age of dinosaurs, to an end.

Postosuchus
237–201 MYA

Caelestiventus
200 MYA

Coelophysis
225–190 MYA

Arizonasaurus
247–242 MYA

Pterodactylus
151–148 MYA

Allosaurus
155–145 MYA

Postosuchus was a large predatory reptile that lived along side the first dinosaurs in late Triassic times.

Arizonasaurus had a tall sail on its back. It was a mid Triassic archosaur, more closely related to crocodiles than to dinosaurs.

Coelophysis was one of the first dinosaurs, Small, slender and fast, it hunted insects and small reptiles.

Caelestiventus was one of the earliest pterosaurs. It lived in North America during the late Triassic.

Kentrosaurus was a stegosaur from Africa. It was about half the size of Stegosaurus and had a mix of plates and spikes along its back as well as two large shoulder spikes.

Pterodactylus lived in Europe and Africa. It was the first flying reptile to be identified as a pterosaur.

Mamenchisaurus is famous for its very long neck. This huge sauropod lived in China.

Allosaurus was a large, fierce predator. Moving on its powerful hind legs, it could run at 35 km/h (21 mph).

Siats meekerorum
About 98 MYA

Hornby Island pterosaurs
About 77 MYA

Styracosaurus
About 75 MYA

Citipati
84–66 MYA

NORTH AMERICA

Many of the most famous dinosaurs lived in North America. Their fossils are most abundant in the deserts and badlands of the West. Fossils keep well in arid conditions, free of plants and soil. They were buried deep, but as the Rocky Mountains rose the fossils were pushed to the surface where scientists could find them.

Continents Adrift

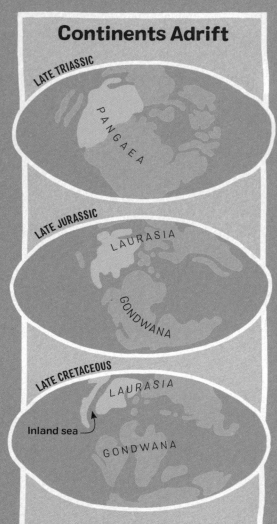

LATE TRIASSIC

PANGAEA

LATE JURASSIC

LAURASIA

GONDWANA

LATE CRETACEOUS

LAURASIA

Inland sea

GONDWANA

The orange lands marked on the maps show what is now North America. During the Cretaceous, the continent was split in two by an inland sea.

Tiny brains
Relative to its size, Stegosaurus had the smallest brain of any dinosaur. It was about the size of a hotdog.

Diplodocus
155–145 MYA

Stegosaurus
155–145 MYA

Triceratops
68–66 MYA

Diplodocus
Like all sauropods, Diplodocus had a long neck and tail, a massive body and four sturdy legs. The long tail was held aloft and could snap like a whip in defence or during mating rituals. Diplodocus lived in large herds and ate a variety of plants.

The largest Tyrannosaurus rex fossil ever found is known as "Scotty." He weighed about 8,900 kg (20,000 lb). Scotty died in Saskatchewan about 66 million years ago when he was 28 years old.

Tyrannosaurus
68–66 MYA

DINORAMA – KNOW IT ALL!
Top 10 North American Facts & Records

1. MOST FAMOUS DINOSAUR
Tyrannosaurus rex, despite recent discoveries of bigger carnivores like Spinosaurus and Giganotosaurus.

2. TWO VERY EARLY NORTH AMERICAN DINOSAURS
Coelophysis and Plateosaurus. Both lived in the late Triassic.

3. DINOSAURS WITH THE HEAVIEST HEADS
Ceratopsids like Triceratops and Styracosaurus because of their huge bony neck frills.

4. DINOSAUR WITH THE LARGEST HEAD CREST
Parasaurolophus. The crest was hollow and up to 1.8 m (6 ft) long.

5. ONE OF THE BIGGEST PTEROSAURS
Quetzalcoatlus. It was about the same size as an F-16 fighter jet.

6. A TYRANNOSAUR RECENTLY DISCOVERED IN A MUSEUM
Thanatotheristes or "Reaper of Death." A close relative of T-Rex. Fossils were found in a museum in Canada in 2018.

7. ONE OF THE LARGEST PLESIOSAURS
Elasmosaurus. It was 15 m (50 ft) long.

8. ONE OF THE TALLEST DINOSAURS
Sauroposeidon. With its head raised it could see inside a six-storey building!

9. DINOSAUR WITH THE THICKEST SKULL
Pachycephalosaurus. Its solid bone skull was up to 26 cm (10 in) thick.

10. A CERATOPSID ABOUT THE SIZE OF A RABBIT
Aquilops.

The powerful jaws were armed with 60 teeth.

The ultimate carnivore
This formidable predator had a mouthful of teeth up to 20 cm (8 in) long, and a jaw grip that was three times that of a modern lion. It used its keen sense of smell to track down its victims, and also to scavenge.

Tyrannosaurus had two long claws on each short forelimb.

Giant Alaskan Troodon
74–65 MYA

Northern dinosaurs
Canada's Dinosaur Provincial Park is the site with the most finds in North America. More than 500 specimens have been found here, representing 40 species.

Plateosaurus
214–204 MYA

Dakotaraptor
71–66 MYA

Caelestiventus
200 MYA

Ornithomimus
74–65 MYA

Western North America has been a rich source of dinosaur fossils. Scientists still regularly discover new species.

Maiasaura
80–75 MYA

Caelestiventus is one of the world's oldest pterosaurs. It's name means "heavenly breeze."

Dinosaur mums
Maiasaura was a duck-billed dinosaur. Its name means "good mother lizard."

Euoplocephalus
76–70 MYA

Deinonychus
120–110 MYA

In the United States, Utah, Wyoming, Colorado and Montana are rich in dinosaur finds. In Canada, Alberta is the state with the most dinosaur fossils.

The Morrison Formation
Centred on Wyoming and Colorado, but sprawling over much of the American West, this late Jurassic layer of sedimentary rock has given up a huge number and variety of dinosaur fossils.

Coelophysis
225–190 MYA

Hesperornithoides
164–145 MYA

Coahuilaceratops
84–71 MYA

Pachycephalosaurus
76–66 MYA

The award for the best preserved Tyrannosaurus fossil goes to "Sue." You can visit Sue at the Field Museum of Natural History, in Chicago.

Coahuilaceratops lived in northern Mexico in the late Cretaceous.

Placerias was a large, late-Triassic herbivore. It lived alongside the first dinosaurs but was unrelated to them.

Elasmosaurus
85–65 MYA

Long-necked sea reptiles
Elasmosaurus was among the longest of the plesiosaurs. It had an especially long neck, with up to 76 vertebrae.

Placerias
221–215 MYA

PREDATORS & PREY

Fierce Allosaurus was a top predator in the late Jurassic. Armed with a jawful of sharp, serrated teeth and powerful hooked claws, it was big enough to take on a fully grown Stegosaurus and may even have attacked the giant sauropods it lived alongside. Stegosaurus was too big and slow to run away, so it used its fearsome spiked tail to defend itself.

Gaping jaws and killer teeth

Allosaurus could open its jaws very wide, delivering devastating wounds with a single bite. Its jaws were lined with more than 70 blade-like teeth.

Allosaurus was one of the earliest dinosaur discoveries. Fossils are plentiful and it is well known. There were several different species.

Flesh-ripping claws

Allosaurus had three sharp claws on each foot to grasp and slash its victims.

Allosaurus	
Lived:	North America, Portugal, Tanzania, Siberia 155–145 MYA
Size:	Length: Up to 12 m (39 ft)
	Weight: 2,300 kg (5,000 lb)
Diet:	Carnivorous

Allosaurus *may have hunted in packs. Working together, they could even bring down a gigantic sauropod.*

30 metres (98 ft)

SAUROPOD HEAVIES

Giants walked the Earth during the age of dinosaurs. Enormous sauropods, such as Diplodocus and Brachiosaurus, roamed the woodlands and plains not just of North America, but all over the world. These are among the largest animals that have ever lived on land. Some weighed more than a dozen elephants. These massive creatures walked on all fours and had column-like legs of solid bone to support their immense weight.

Plateosaurus *was a prosauropod. It was an ancestor of the huge sauropods and still walked on two legs.*

Diplodocus *had comb-like teeth which it used to strip the needles off conifer trees.*

Supersaurus *was one of the largest of them all. It survived into the early Cretaceous period.*

Plateosaurus
214–204 MYA

Diplodocus
155–145 MYA

Supersaurus
157–142 MYA

Brachiosaur
155–140 MYA

The thagomizer

Stegosaurus had four sharp spikes on the end of its tail which it used for defence. The spiked tail is called a thagomizer.

Stegosaurus

Lived:	North America, Portugal 155–145 MYA
Size:	Length: 8–9 m (26–30 ft)
	Weight: Up to 3,000 kg (6,600 lb)
Diet:	Herbivorous

Why did Stegosaurus have plates?

The plates were too thin and fragile for defence. They were criss-crossed with blood vessels so they may have helped to keep Stegosaurus cool. They may also have been used for display, to attract mates at breeding time.

The most complete Stegosaurus skeleton is in the Natural History Museum in London. Affectionately known as Sophie, she has helped scientists learn a lot about these hulking creatures.

Brachiosaurus *had a crest-like feature on its head.*

Camarsaurus *was one of the most common sauropods during the late Jurassic.*

Apatosaurus *had such a long neck that early scientists thought that it lived under water!*

Sauroposeidon *is only known from a few fossils. It was possibly the tallest dinosaur that ever lived.*

Alamosaurus *lived millions of years after the other sauropods in North America had disappeared.*

18 m (59 ft)

Camarasaurus
155–145 MYA

Apatosaurus
152–151 MYA

Barosaurus
152–150 MYA

Sauroposeidon
125–100 MYA

Alamosaurus
70–66 MYA

SKULL CRESTS

Parasaurolophus lived alongside the ceratopsids, but was not closely related to them. It was a hadrosaur, or duck-billed dinosaur, and had a beak-like mouth and a tall crest on the back of its skull. Parasaurolophus was bipedal and quadrupedal (walked on two legs and four) and fed on a variety of plants.

Parasaurolophus
77–73 MYA

The crest was used for display, or to tell other dinosaurs about an individual's species and sex. It may also have been used to amplify calls.

The crest was hollow, with tubes running from the nostrils to the top of the crest and back.

Male Pachycephalosaurus used their thick skulls in head-butting contests during the mating season.

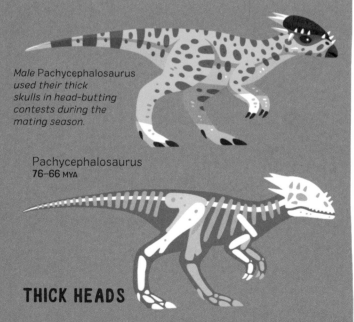

Pachycephalosaurus
76–66 MYA

THICK HEADS

Pachycephalosaurus means "thick-headed" and these plant-eating dinosaurs had bony domes on their heads that were at least 26 cm (10 in) thick. Just one species is known from fossils found in Montana, South Dakota and Wyoming.

HORNS & FRILLS

Late Cretaceous North America was home to a family of dinosaurs with wildly elaborate arrays of horns and bony frills on their skulls. These were the ceratopsids. The most famous family member was Triceratops, but there were dozens of different species, each with its own amazing line-up of horns and frills.

Why did they have fancy frills?
The most likely explanation is that the ornate headgear was to attract mates. Both males and females had them and a good display showed that an individual was healthy and a good partner to choose.

The ceratopsids were divided into two groups. The chasmosaurines had long, triangular frills and big horns on their brows. The centrosaurines had rectangular frills with spikes and horns on their snouts.

Aquilops was one of the earliest American ceratopsids. It was the size of a rabbit.

Styracosaurus
83–70 MYA

Styracosaurus had one of the most impressive displays. Each individual had a slightly different frill and horns.

Kosmoceratops
84–71 MYA

Aquilops
108–104 MYA

Wendiceratops
79–78 MYA

Centrosaurus
76–75 MYA

Chasmosaurus
83–70 MYA

Utahceratops
76–75 MYA

Einosaurus
84–72 MYA

Albertaceratops
83–76 MYA

Hellboy (Regaliceratops)

Lived: USA, 68 MYA

Length: 5 m (16.4 ft)

Weight: 1,500 kg (3300 lb)

Diet: Herbivorous

Hellboy is a new species of ceratopsid dinosaur that is closely related to Triceratops. Its huge bony frill was topped with spikes like a crown, and its head weighed more than 265 kg (590 lb).

QUETZALCOATLUS

This giant predatory pterosaur stalked its prey on the plains of North America for four million years. Moving stealthily on all fours, it used its fearsome beak to snap up smaller reptiles, including young or sick dinosaurs. Quetzalcoatlus was equally at home in the sky, where it soared on currents of air like an outsize hang glider.

PTEROSAURS AROUND THE WORLD

Pterosaurs were flying reptiles that lived alongside the dinosaurs. The two groups were close cousins that evolved on separate branches of the reptile family tree.

Sordes *was a small pterosaur from late-Jurassic Kazakhstan.*

Sordes
163–152 MYA

Jeholopterus *lived in China. It is known as the "vampire pterosaur" because it may have sucked the blood of dinosaurs.*

Jeholopterus
165–161 MYA

Thalassodromeus
112–109 MYA

Thalassodromeus *lived in Brazil. It had a huge crest on its skull and toothless jaws.*

Quetzalcoatlus

Lived:	North America, 71–66 MYA
Size:	Wingspan: 10–12 m (33–39 ft)
Weight:	Disputed, but probably about 250 kg (550 lb)
Diet:	Carnivorous (small dinosaurs & other reptiles)

Some scientists think that Quetzalcoatlus *was too heavy to fly, but most believe that it could vault into the air using its powerful limbs. Once airborne, it could soar and glide at speeds of up to 90 km/h (56 mph).*

At first, palaeontologists thought that Quetzalcoatlus *fed on fish by skimming over the surface of the sea like many smaller pterosaurs. But* Quetzalcoatlus *was far too big to hunt this way. It is more likely that it hunted on the ground, capturing small reptiles or baby dinosaurs like these Triceratops.*

Nyctosaurus was about the size of a modern bald eagle. Like the eagles, it fed on fish and anything else it could scrounge.

Nyctosaurus
89–66 MYA

Nyctosaurus

Lived:	North America, 89–66 MYA
Size:	Wingspan: 3 m (10 ft)
Weight:	About 9 kg (20 lb)
Diet:	Piscivore (fish)

Nyctosaurus *had a large v-shaped head crest.*

Quetzalcoatlus belonged to a family of Cretaceous pterosaurs called azhdarchids. These were the largest flying reptiles, and probably the biggest animals ever to take to the skies.

Over 1,000 Pteranodon fossils have been found, making it one of the best known pterosaurs. The males had large head crests, probably used during courtship and territorial disputes.

Pteranodon
90–70 MYA

Quetzalcoatlus is named for the Aztec god Quetzalcoatl, or "the feathered serpent." In reality, like all pterosaurs, Quetzalcoatlus did not have feathers.

In flight, the Pteranodon *moved like an albatross, soaring on air currents and only flapping its wings occasionally.*

Pteranodon

Lived:	North America, 90–70 MYA
Size:	Wingspan: 7 m (23 ft)
Weight:	Disputed, probably about 40 kg (88 lb)
Diet:	Piscivore (fish)

Quetzalcoatlus stood as tall as a giraffe. Its wingspan of 10–12 metres (33–39 ft), was as large as that of a light aircraft.

SOUTH AMERICA

Eodromaeus
237–228 MYA

South America has some of the oldest dinosaur fossils. Palaeontologists believe that the first dinosaurs evolved here during the Triassic, at least 240 million years ago. At that time all the land on Earth was united in a supercontinent called Pangaea and early dinosaurs were free to roam all over. When Pangaea split in two, dinosaurs in northern Laurasia began to evolve in different ways from those in southern Gondwana.

South America was home to many of the largest dinosaurs that have ever walked the Earth. Titanosaurs like Argentinosaurus, Dreadnoughtus and Futalognkosaurus all lived here.

Continents Adrift

LATE TRIASSIC

PANGAEA

LATE JURASSIC

LAURASIA

GONDWANA

LATE CRETACEOUS

LAURASIA

GONDWANA

The orange lands marked on the maps above show what is now South America. During the Triassic and Jurassic, South America was joined to Africa. The two continents have many dinosaurs in common.

Titanosaurs
Named for a battleship, Dreadnoughtus was at least six medium-large car lengths long and weighed more than 12 African elephants. Futalognkosaurus was even longer.

Futalognkosaurus
93–85 MYA

Eoraptor
231–228 MYA

Dreadnoughtus
84–66 MYA

Riojasaurus
228–208 MYA

Austroraptor
85–66 MYA

Southern raptor
Austroraptor had the dromaeosaur's trademark and deadly sickle-shaped claw on its hind limbs. It differs from other raptors in that its teeth and jaws suggest that it hunted fish as well as small mammals and pterosaurs. Austraptor had a covering of feathers.

At 5 metres (16 ft) long and weighing about 300 kg (660 lb), Austroraptor was the largest dromaeosaur in the Southern Hemisphere, on a par with Dakotaraptor and Utahraptor in North America.

DINORAMA - KNOW IT ALL!
Top 10 South American Dinosaur Facts & Records

1. WORLD'S LONGEST DINOSAUR
Argentinosaurus. It was up to 40 metres (131 ft) long. That's about nine car lengths!

2. LARGEST CARNIVOROUS DINOSAUR IN SOUTH AMERICA
Giganotosaurus. Bigger and faster than T-Rex, this scary predator lived 30 million years before its more famous North American cousin.

3. ONE OF THE EARLIEST DINOSAURS IN SOUTH AMERICA
Eoraptor, or "dawn thief."

4. DINOSAUR WITH LONG NECK SPIKES
Amargasaurus. It had 60-cm (24-in) long, forward-facing spikes on its neck and looked truly bizarre.

5. BRAZILIAN PTEROSAUR WITH LARGE BONY HEAD CREST
Caiuajara. Found in massive bonebed in 1971.

6. DINOSAUR NAMED FOR A BATTLESHIP
Dreadnoughtus. It was so big it took scientists four summers to dig up the skeleton.

7. DINOSAUR HEAD SCANNED IN A CT SCANNER
Gnathovorax. It was 233 million years old but in good condition.

8. REPTILES THAT ARE THE ANCESTORS OF MODERN MAMMALS
Cynodonts. Lived 260–176 MYA.

9. STRANGEST DINOSAUR NAME
Irritator. Scientists were "irritated" by fossil dealers who had added cement to its snout.

10. TITANOSAUR COVERED ALL OVER WITH BONY BODY PLATES
Saltosaurus.

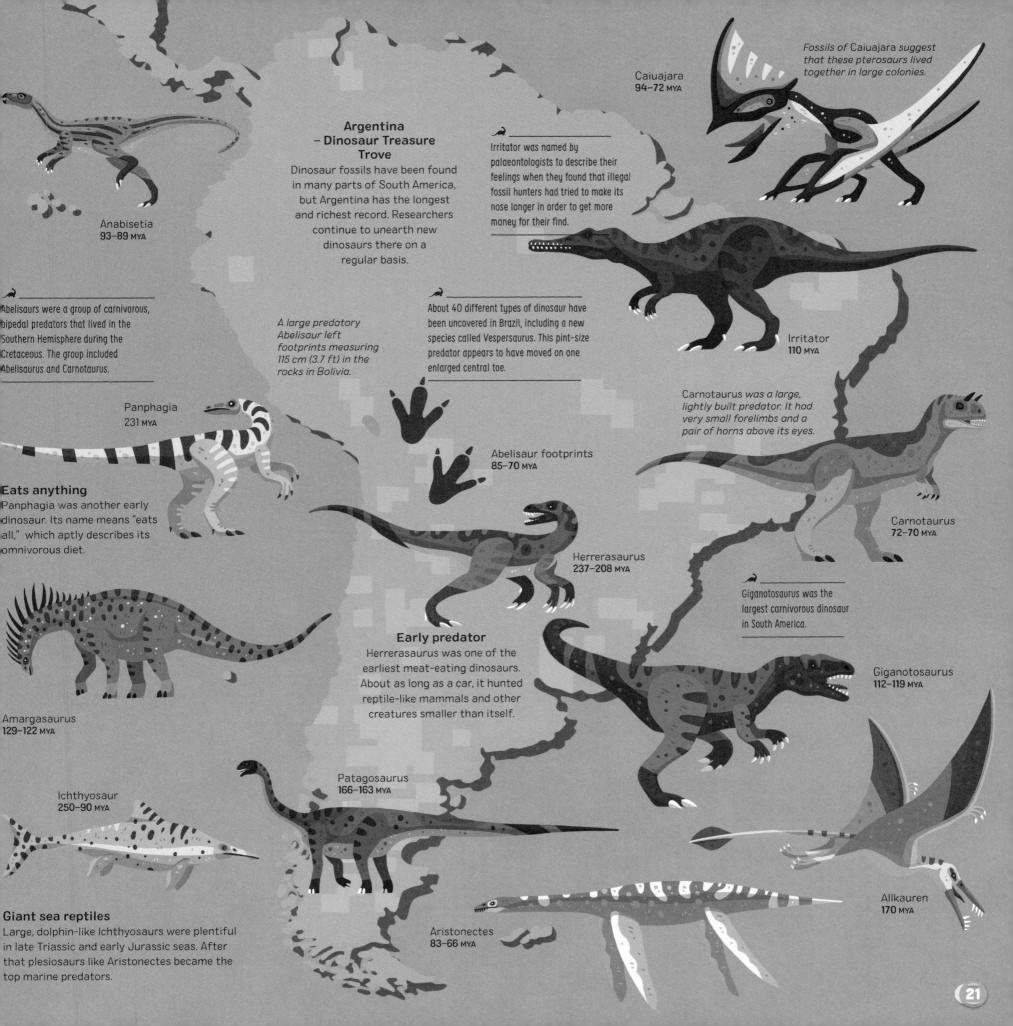

Anabisetia
93–89 MYA

Argentina – Dinosaur Treasure Trove

Dinosaur fossils have been found in many parts of South America, but Argentina has the longest and richest record. Researchers continue to unearth new dinosaurs there on a regular basis.

Irritator was named by palaeontologists to describe their feelings when they found that illegal fossil hunters had tried to make its nose longer in order to get more money for their find.

Fossils of Caiuajara suggest that these pterosaurs lived together in large colonies.

Caiuajara
94–72 MYA

Abelisaurs were a group of carnivorous, bipedal predators that lived in the Southern Hemisphere during the Cretaceous. The group included Abelisaurus and Carnotaurus.

A large predatory Abelisaur left footprints measuring 115 cm (3.7 ft) in the rocks in Bolivia.

About 40 different types of dinosaur have been uncovered in Brazil, including a new species called Vespersaurus. This pint-size predator appears to have moved on one enlarged central toe.

Irritator
110 MYA

Panphagia
231 MYA

Eats anything
Panphagia was another early dinosaur. Its name means "eats all," which aptly describes its omnivorous diet.

Abelisaur footprints
85–70 MYA

Carnotaurus was a large, lightly built predator. It had very small forelimbs and a pair of horns above its eyes.

Carnotaurus
72–70 MYA

Herrerasaurus
237–208 MYA

Early predator
Herrerasaurus was one of the earliest meat-eating dinosaurs. About as long as a car, it hunted reptile-like mammals and other creatures smaller than itself.

Giganotosaurus was the largest carnivorous dinosaur in South America.

Giganotosaurus
112–119 MYA

Amargasaurus
129–122 MYA

Patagosaurus
166–163 MYA

Ichthyosaur
250–90 MYA

Allkauren
170 MYA

Giant sea reptiles
Large, dolphin-like Ichthyosaurs were plentiful in late Triassic and early Jurassic seas. After that plesiosaurs like Aristonectes became the top marine predators.

Aristonectes
83–66 MYA

BEFORE THE DINOSAURS

Dinosaurs didn't just suddenly appear. They evolved from earlier reptiles over long periods of time. Dinosaurs were part of a group of animals called archosaurs, which still exist today as crocodiles and birds. When dinosaurs first appeared, there were many different types of archosaurs.

Pisanosaurus
228–216 MYA

Dinosaur or not?

Pisanosaurus is known from a very incomplete skeleton found in Argentina in 1962. At first scientists thought it was an early dinosaur, but now they think it was a silesaurid — a close relative of the first dinosaurs.

Ischigualastia
237–227 MYA

Ischigualastia was a very large dicynodont. It was much bigger than its better-known relative Placerias. Ischigualastia moved on four legs and ate plants. Dicynodonts all died out at the end of the Triassic.

Saurosuchus
237–208 MYA

Saurosuchus means "lizard crocodile" and it is an apt name for this huge, deadly predator. Saurosuchus lived alongside small early dinosaurs like Herrerasaurus and Eoraptor, although it would have been too slow to capture them.

TRIASSIC TERROR

A recent fossil find in Brazil revealed a stunning new predatory dinosaur, possibly the first ever to have terrorized the Earth. Gnathovorax, which means "ravenous jaws," was a horse-size carnivore that hunted creatures such as rhynchosaurs and cynodonts. The fossilised skeleton was in such good condition that scientists were able to put the head in a CT scanner to learn about the ancient dinosaur's brain.

Cynodonts

This large group of warm-blooded, hairy animals existed long before the dinosaurs. They are the ancestors of modern mammals, including humans. Their name means "dog teeth."

Menadon was a cynodont about the size of a large dog. It probably looked a bit like a big rodent. Here it flees from a hungry Gnathovorax.

Menadon
250–200 MYA

THE SEARCH FOR THE FIRST DINOSAURS

The closest relatives to dinosaurs have been identified as the silesaurids, which were medium-size animals that looked like long-legged lizards. But there is a gap of about 10–15 million years between the silesaurids and the first true dinosaurs. Scientists are searching for clues to fill this gap.

Marasuchus
242–237 MYA

Saturnalia
237–208 MYA

Saturnalia was a very early dinosaur that had traits of both sauropod and theropod dinosaurs.

Marasuchus was an archosaur that had many but not all of the adaptations that define a dinosaur. Its name means "Mara crocodile."

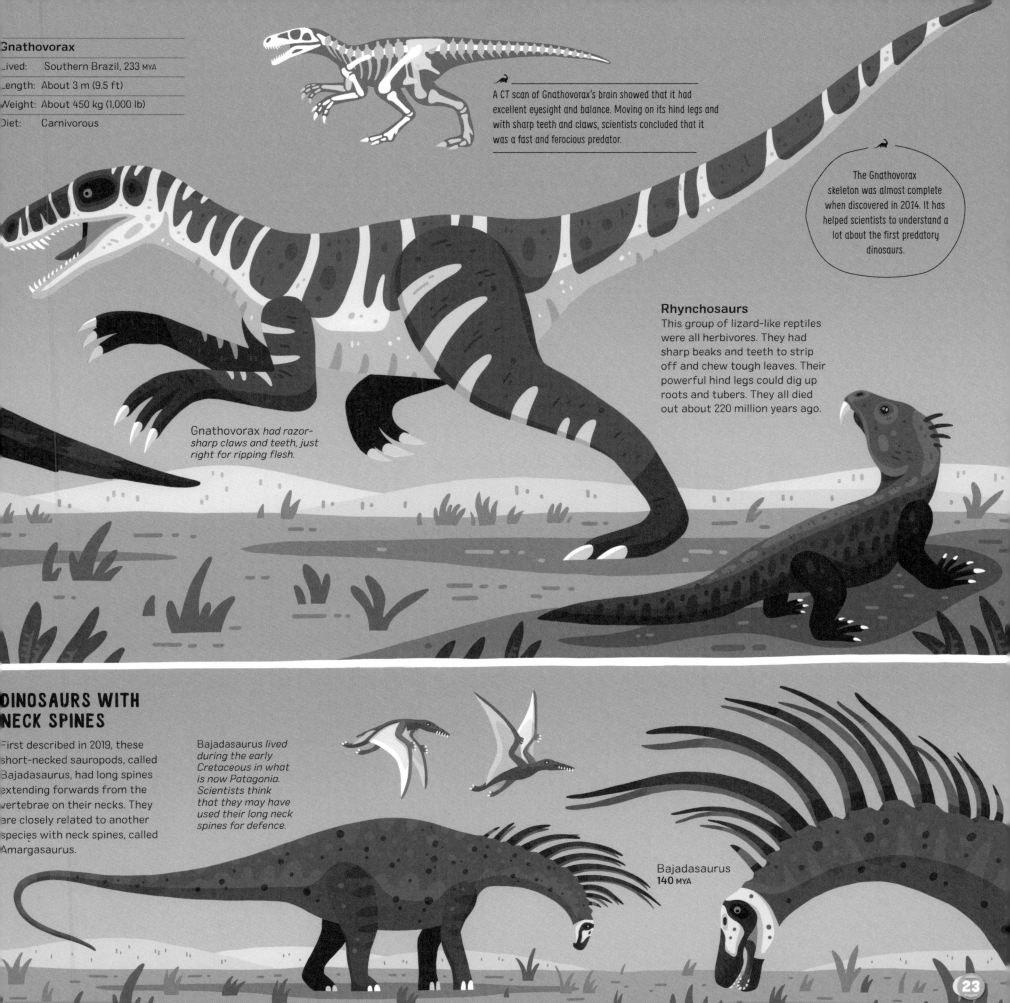

Gnathovorax

Lived:	Southern Brazil, 233 MYA
Length:	About 3 m (9.5 ft)
Weight:	About 450 kg (1,000 lb)
Diet:	Carnivorous

A CT scan of Gnathovorax's brain showed that it had excellent eyesight and balance. Moving on its hind legs and with sharp teeth and claws, scientists concluded that it was a fast and ferocious predator.

The Gnathovorax skeleton was almost complete when discovered in 2014. It has helped scientists to understand a lot about the first predatory dinosaurs.

Gnathovorax *had razor-sharp claws and teeth, just right for ripping flesh.*

Rhynchosaurs
This group of lizard-like reptiles were all herbivores. They had sharp beaks and teeth to strip off and chew tough leaves. Their powerful hind legs could dig up roots and tubers. They all died out about 220 million years ago.

DINOSAURS WITH NECK SPINES

First described in 2019, these short-necked sauropods, called Bajadasaurus, had long spines extending forwards from the vertebrae on their necks. They are closely related to another species with neck spines, called Amargasaurus.

Bajadasaurus *lived during the early Cretaceous in what is now Patagonia. Scientists think that they may have used their long neck spines for defence.*

Bajadasaurus
140 MYA

CLASH OF THE TITANS

Many of the largest dinosaurs lived in South America, especially during the Cretaceous period. Some, like the giant titanosaurs, were herbivores, while others, such as Giganotosaurus, were predatory carnivores. Some scientists think South American dinosaurs grew really big because the continent was isolated from the rest of the world. The biggest titanosaurs were longer than blue whales (the largest creatures on Earth today), but not as heavy.

Titanosaur bodies

Titanosaurs were large herbivores with long necks and tails. They were sturdier than other sauropods. Some even had armoured plates on their bodies.

Argentinosaurus

Lived:	Argentina, 99–90 MYA
Length:	Up to 35 m (115 ft)
Weight:	Up to 100,000 kg (220,000 lb)
Diet:	Herbivorous

On the defence

Argentinosaurus was a very big animal. Even if working as a pack, Giganotosaurus would have found it difficult to bring down a healthy adult. They probably waited and watched the giant sauropods, on the lookout for elderly, sick or young individuals.

Giganotosaurus had 20-cm (8-in) sharp, pointy teeth that could slash through the tough skins of its prey.

Giganotosaurus

Lived:	Argentina, 112–90 MYA
Length:	Up to 13 m (43 ft)
Weight:	Up to 14,000 kg (31,000 lb)
Diet:	Carnivorous

Notocolossus *fossils show that titanosaurs had specially adapted feet to carry their immense weight, allowing them to grow as large as they did.*

Titanosaurs

The titanosaurs were the last of the huge sauropods that first appeared in the Jurassic. There were more than 60 species and they lived in Africa, Asia, South America, Europe and Australia. The largest titanosaurs, including Argentinosaurus, Patagotitan and Dread-noughtus, all lived in South America.

Patagotitan *was very large. It was closely related to Argentinosaurus and was probably longer but not quite as sturdy.*

Saltasaurus *was one of the smaller titanosaurs, although it was still bigger and heavier than a modern African elephant. It had bony plates embedded in its skin.*

Patagotitan
102–95 MYA

Saltasaurus
70-66 MYA

Notocolossus
89–83 MYA

[Ar]gentinosaurus *probably lived in [h]erds much as herbivores do today. [T]hey would have helped to defend [e]ach other in case of attack.*

On the attack

Giganotosaurus was part of the carcharodontosaur (shark-toothed lizard) family. It lived 30 million years before Tyrannosaurus rex, but was larger and at least as powerful. Giganotosaurus was the top predator in its environment for almost two million years.

Giganotosaurus *could move at about 50 km/h (30 mph) and used its tail for balance.*

[Ar]gentinosaurus survived right up until the end [of] the dinosaur age when the Cretaceous—[Pa]leogene extinction event wiped out all [no]n-avian dinosaurs.

Continents Adrift

LATE TRIASSIC

PANGAEA

LATE JURASSIC

LAURASIA

GONDWANA

LATE CRETACEOUS

LAURASIA

GONDWANA

The orange lands on these maps show what is now Europe. During the Mesozoic much of Europe was made up of scattered islands in warm, shallow seas.

The earliest dinosaurs in Europe date to 225 million years ago. About 80 species have been found at hundreds of locations across the continent. Dinosaurs lived in most European countries, but England, Portugal, Spain, France, Germany and Romania have the richest fossil sites.

The biggest carnivore
Torvosaurus is the largest predatory dinosaur ever found in Europe. It had long, sharp teeth and claws for ripping flesh. Torvosaurus lived in Portugal and France and may have had a light coating of fuzzy feathers.

An early pterosaur
Eudimorphodon was one of the earliest pterosaurs. It was found in northern Italy. Flying over the shallow seas, it snatched insects from the air and fish from the sea.

Eudimorphodon
215–201 MYA

Torvosaurus
155–144 MYA

Balaur
72–66 MYA

Balaur had two retractable, sickle-shaped claws on each hind foot.

Magyarosaurus
83–66 MYA

Island of the dwarf dinosaurs
Balaur and Magyarosaurus lived on an island called Hateg in the Tethys Sea, now part of modern Romania. All the dinosaurs on Hateg were smaller than their continental cousins. Balaur belonged to the group of dinosaurs that evolved into modern birds. Magyarosaurus was a relatively small sauropod.

DINORAMA – KNOW IT ALL!
Top 10 European Dinosaur Facts & Records

1. LARGEST KNOWN PREDATORY DINOSAUR IN EUROPE
Torvosaurus. At 12 metres (39 ft), it was longer than a big city bus.

2. ONE OF THE EARLIEST PTEROSAURS
Eudimophodon. It had over 100 teeth in its tiny jaws.

3. EUROPEAN DINOSAUR THAT SHOWS THE LINK BETWEEN DINOSAURS AND BIRDS
Archaeopteryx. It shows a transitional phase between dinosaurs and birds.

4. MARINE REPTILES THAT REPLACED ICYTHYOSAURS AS TOP SEA PREDATORS
Mososaurs. About 90 MYA.

5. AN EARLY CRETACEOUS PREDATOR FROM ENGLAND
Neovenator. Slim and fast, it was a top predator of its time.

6. TWO DWARF DINOSAURS FROM HATEG ISLAND IN ROMANIA
Balaur and Magyarosaurus.

7. REPTILES THAT DIDN'T LAY EGGS
Ichthyosaurs. These marine reptiles gave birth to live young.

8. DINOSAUR WHOSE APPEARANCE WAS MISUNDERSTOOD FOR DECADES
Iguanadon. Its thumb spike was placed on its snout like a horn!

9. WHAT IS A PLESIOSAUR WITH A SHORT NECK IS CALLED?
A pliosaur. They had short, crocodile-like necks and were very fierce.

10. THE EARLIEST KNOWN TURTLE
Proganochelys. It was about 1 metre (3 ft) long and looked like a modern turtle.

Ophthalmosaurus
165–160 MYA

Triassic herbivore
Plateosaurus fossils have been found in more than 50 places in Europe, making it one of the best-known dinosaurs. Its sharp, leaf-shaped teeth were ideal for slicing through tough plant fibres. Plateosaurus moved on two legs, using its tail for balance.

Plateosaurus
214–204 MYA

Little-horned face
Leptoceratops was a small ceratopsid dinosaur that lived in Scandinavia and North America. It was so small it could have walked under Triceratops' belly.

Leptoceratops
67–66 MYA

Although Europe is not the richest source of dinosaur fossils, it was here that dinosaurs were first discovered and named.

Polish dragon
Smok ("dragon" in Polish), was a large predatory archosaur, or dinosaur ancestor. It had big, sturdy teeth for crushing the bones of its prey.

Megalosaurus
170–155 MYA

Smok
About 210 MYA

Sciurumimus
155–150 MYA

Iguanodon
157–94 MYA

Neovenator
133–125 MYA

Struthiosaurus
83–66 MYA

Notatessoraeraptor
About 210 MYA

The word "dinosaur" was coined by British scientist Richard Owen in 1842. Dinosaur fossils were known before that time but Owens was the first to recognise them as a group.

Baryonx
145–125 MYA

Miragaia
155–145 MYA

Scipionyx
112–109 MYA

Mistralazhdarcho
About 75 MYA

Cymbospindylus
240–210 MYA

27

IGUANODON WORLD

The first Iguanodon fossils were discovered in England in 1822. They were one of the earliest dinosaurs to be named. These large herbivores were common across much of Europe during the early Cretaceous. Many complete skeletons have been found and Iguanodons are one of the better known dinosaur species.

Iguanodon

Lived:	Europe, 157–94 MYA
Length:	Up to 10 m (33 ft)
Weight:	Up to 5,000 kg (11,000 lb)
Diet:	Herbivorous

Treacherous habitat
Iguanodons lived in marshy areas full of treacherous quicksands and predatory reptiles. Fully grown Iguanodons stood almost three metres (10 ft) tall and weighed up to 6,000 kg (13,200 lb), so even the largest carnivores would not have attacked them, but young, sick and elderly individuals were at risk.

Fierce crocodile-like Goniopholis lurked in the shallow waters and on swampy banks ready to make a meal of any stray Iguanodon youngsters.

The large, meat-eating allosaurid dinosaur Neovenator was common in Europe during the early Cretaceous. Working in a pack of three of more, these large predators may even have dared to attack adult Iguanodons.

ARCHAEOPTERYX – AN EARLY BIRD

The well-preserved skeleton of this small creature was discovered in Germany in 1861. About the size of a large crow, and with feathers and wings, it looked very like a bird. But it also had jaws, teeth and a tail, which no modern birds have. Its discovery set off a furious scientific debate about whether it was a dinosaur, or a bird, or something in between.

Archaeopteryx

Lived:	Europe, About 150 MYA
Length:	About 50 cm (19.5 in)
Weight:	About 1 kg (2 lb)
Diet:	Carnivorous

Archaeopteryx was a carnivore, feeding on small reptiles, mammals and insects. It had strong jaws and sharp teeth and claws to catch and hold prey.

Archaeopteryx was one of the most important fossils ever found. Most scientists now believe that it represents a transitional phase of reptiles as they evolved into birds.

When you look at the skeleton of Archaeopteryx it is very easy to see why scientists immediately linked it to birds.

Askeptosaurus *fossils from the mid Triassic have been found in Italy and Switzerland. It had webbed feet and lived close to the shoreline where it hunted fish.*

Askeptosaurus
247–225 MYA

Sea turtles
The ancestors of modern sea turtles evolved about 110 MYA. They included Archelon, the largest turtle ever known.

Proganochelys
228–201 MYA

Proganochelys *is one of the oldest turtles known. It may have lived in shallow seas or on land.*

MARINE REPTILES

While dinosaurs ruled on land, many different types of reptiles lived in the seas. There were at least 12 groups of marine reptiles, including plesiosaurs, sea turtles, ichthyosaurs, mosasaurs and marine crocodiles. The warm seas that covered much of Europe were home to many of these creatures throughout the Mesozoic.

MOSASAURS
When ichthyosaurs went extinct, mosasaurs took over as the ruling group of marine reptiles. They were ferocious predators with sharp, spiked teeth for holding and biting prey.

Mosasaurs *didn't have gills so they stayed near the surface to breath, in the same way that whales do today.*

ICHTHYOSAURS

Members of this large group looked a lot like dolphins. Their name means "fish lizards." They were the top sea predators for 150 million years. They died out about 30 million years before the dinosaurs.

Young ichthyosaurs were born live and looked exactly like their parents, only smaller.

Giant ichthyosaur discovery
A man walking his dogs in Somerset, UK, found the bone of an ichthyosaur that may have been larger than any previously known species. It was almost as big as a blue whale, the largest known creature ever to have lived on Earth.

New giant ichthyosaur

Lived:	UK, 205 MYA
Length:	26 m (85 ft)
Weight:	Up to 100,000 kg (220,000 lb)
Diet:	Carnivorous

> The first ichthyosaur skeleton to be correctly identified was found by a young English fossil hunter named Mary Anning. She was just 12 at the time.

PLESIOSAURS

Plesiosaurs were a large group of predatory, meat-eating marine reptiles that lived from the late Triassic until the end of the Cretaceous. More than 100 species have been described. Plesiosaurs gave birth to live young, breathed air and may even have been warm-blooded. They are divided into two main groups according to the length of their necks.

Short-necked pliosaurs
Plesiosaurs with short, crocodile-like necks and large heads are known as pliosaurs. They were fast and lethal, actively hunting sharks, fish, squid and other marine reptiles.

Long-necked plesiosaurs
These creatures had long necks, small heads and large flippers to propel themselves along. They were slow-moving and fed on fish and other small animals.

Liopleurodon lived in the second half of the Jurassic. At 9 metres (30 ft) long, it was big, but not the biggest pliosaur. Other species grew to 15 metres (50 ft).

Liopleurodon
166–140 MYA

Plesiosaurus
199–175 MYA

Plesiosaurus lived during the first half of the Jurassic. It was a medium-size plesiosaur, growing to 3–5 metres (10–16 ft) long. Some others, like the Antarctic Elasmosaur on page 45, were much bigger.

Mosasaurus

Lived:	Seas worldwide, 82–66 MYA
Length:	18 m (60 ft)
Weight:	14,000 kg (31,000 lb)
Diet:	Carnivorous

Mosasaurus hunted fish, including sharks, smaller marine reptiles, birds and pterosaurs. Its double-hinged jaw allowed it to swallow prey whole.

MARINE CROCODILES

Shaped like modern crocodiles, these crocodylomorphs lived on land and in the sea during the late Jurassic and early Cretaceous. They were all active hunters.

Machimosaurus hugi
About 160 MYA

Machimosaurus hugi was almost as long as a bus. It was one of the largest marine crocodiles, and a fearsome predator.

Continents Adrift

PANGAEA

LAURASIA

GONDWANA

LAURASIA

GONDWANA

India

The orange lands marked on the maps above show what is now Asia. India did not drift north to join Asia until about 45 million years ago, long after the dinosaurs had died out.

ASIA

China and Mongolia are hot spots for dinosaur finds. Vast areas of desert and sedimentary rock have yielded spectacular fossils over the past 25 years that have changed the way we think about dinosaur life and evolution. India also has some invaluable fossils that developed separately because the subcontinent only joined Asia long after the end of the dinosaur age.

Liaoning treasure trove

From the mid 1990s, sensational finds in Liaoning, in northeastern China, proved that dinosaurs were the ancestors of modern birds, resolving a long-running scientific dispute. Many other key discoveries have also been made there.

Gigantspinosaurus
163–157 MYA

With its huge shoulder spikes, Gigantspinosaurus was an amazing sight. This early Chinese stegosaur had smaller spines and plates along its back than later stegosaurs.

Protoceratops
80–75 MYA

Protoceratops was about the size of a sheep. One of its ancestors migrated to North America where its descendants evolved into the many ceratopsid dinosaurs (see pages 16–17).

Zhenyuanlong
About 125 MYA

Zhenyuanlong was a fast predatory raptor with a full coat of feathers. It had large wings but could not fly. About 2 metres (6 ft) long, it looked a lot like a bird. It was closely related to Velociraptor.

DINORAMA – KNOW IT ALL!
Top 10 Asian Dinosaur Facts & Records

1. FIRST NON-AVIAN FEATHERED DINOSAUR
Sinosauropteryx. Its discovery in 1996 changed the way we view dinosaurs.

2. WORLD'S LARGEST DUCK-BILLED DINOSAUR
Shantungosaurus. Lived in China and weighed up to 16,000 kg (35,000 lb).

3. A DUCK-BILLED DINOSAUR FROM JAPAN
Kamuysaurus. Lived on Hokkaido.

4. AN EARLY ASIAN COUSIN OF TRICERATOPS
Protoceratops. Lived in Mongolia and northern China.

5. THE MOST FAMOUS ASIAN DINOSAUR
Velociraptor.

6. STEGOSAUR WITH GIANT SHOULDER SPIKES
Gigantspinosaurus. It used the spikes for defence and display.

7. A VERY IMPORTANT FOSSIL REGION IN CHINA
Liaoning Province. There are now at least ten museums in the region.

8. DINOSAUR WITH A VERY LONG NECK
Mamenchisaurus. Its neck could stretch to 10 metres (33 ft), or almost as long as a bus.

9. DINOSAURS WITH THE LONGEST CLAWS OF ANY KNOWN ANIMAL
Therizinosaurus.

10. FOSSILS OF BABY DINOSAURS FOUND HUDDLING TOGETHER FOR WARMTH AND COMFORT.
Oviraptor in the Gobi Desert. The discovery shows that dinosaurs had social lives.

Plant-eating sauropods had the longest necks of any animal. Mamenchisaurus had one of the longest necks of them all. It made up nearly half its body length.

Mamenchisaurus

Lived:	China, 160–145 MYA
Size:	Length: 20 m (66 ft)
	Weight: 2,700 kg (6,000 lb)
Diet:	Herbivorous

The Giant Mongolian pterosaur *found in the Gobi Desert may have been as large as Quetzalcoatlus (see pages 18–19). It feasted on baby dinosaurs.*

Microraptor lived 25 million years after Europe's Archaeopteryx. Scientists believe that dinosaurs evolved into bird-like creatures more than once during the Mesozoic.

Microraptor was tiny — about the size of a pigeon. It had four wings and feathers.

Microraptor
125–113 MYA

Giant Mongolian pterosaur
About 70 MYA

Kulindadromeus
174–145 MYA

Crow-size Anchiornis had feathers and four wings. One of the earliest bird-like dinosaurs, it is well known because so many fossils have been found.

Timurlenga
94–90 MYA

Dilong
128–127 MYA

Anchiornis
168–151 MYA

Velociraptor was made famous by the Jurassic Park films. However, it didn't live in North America, but in the Gobi Desert in Mongolia where it was discovered in the 1920s.

Velociraptor
75–71 MYA

Kamuysaurus
72–70 MYA

Tyrannosaurid
167–161 MYA

Lingwulong
About 174 MYA

Shantungosaurus
80–66 MYA

Lufengosaurus
201–191 MYA

Barapasaurus
199–183 MYA

Mamenchisaurus
163–140 MYA

Isanosaurus
About 210 MYA

Oculudentavis, the smallest dinosaur ever found, lived in Myanmar around 100 MYA. It weighed about 2 g (0.07 oz) and was around the same size as the bee hummingbird — the world's smallest bird.

Alwalkeria
237–208 MYA

Alwalkeria was a very early dinosaur from India. It ate insects, small vertebrates and plants.

Cartorhynchus
About 248 MYA

Early "fish lizards"
Cartorhynchus was only about 40 cm (16 in) long and lived at the beginning of the Triassic. It was an early form of ichthyosaur ("fish lizard" in Greek).

Cartorhynchus had flippers that may also have been used for walking on land.

FEATHERED DINOSAURS

Most dinosaur fossils are of hard bones and teeth but occasionally fossils of soft body parts are found. The discovery in China of many small theropod dinosaurs with feathers was a stunning breakthrough. Palaeontologists had proof that these extinct dinosaurs looked very like living birds, supporting the theory that birds are small, flying dinosaurs.

Sinosauropteryx
130–120 MYA

Sinosauropteryx, *discovered in Liaoning in 1996, was the first Asian dinosaur with feathers. Its feathers were primitive and more like fuzz or hair than modern bird feathers. They also revealed that Sinosauropteryx was probably orange with a striped tail.*

Caudipteryx
130–122 MYA

Caudipteryx *was also found in Liaoning. It was about the size of a peacock and its feathers were like those of modern birds. The feathers on its arms and tail were long but it could not fly. They were used for warmth and to attract mates.*

Yutyrannus
130–113 MYA

Yutyrannus *was a tryrannosaurid dinosaur from Liaoning and a primitive cousin of Tyrannosaurus rex. At 10 metres (33 ft) long and 3 metres (10 ft) tall, it is the largest feathered dinosaur ever found.*

SOCIAL LIVES

When researchers realised that dinosaurs were a lot like modern birds, they began to look for evidence of similar behaviour. We know that many dinosaurs lived together in groups and some nested in large colonies. Fossilised tracks show that individuals walked together, perhaps in family groups or hunting parties.

What a sight!
Gigantoraptor looked like a very large bird, although scientists aren't sure if it had a full covering of feathers. The male and female Gigantoraptors may have danced together in mating rituals like those of modern birds.

Gigantoraptor was an oviraptosaur but was huge compared to others in the group.

Gigantoraptor's *large horny beak was toothless, ideal for crushing and grinding tough plant fibres.*

Gigantoraptor

Lived:	Mongolia, 83–70 MYA
Length:	8 m (26 ft)
Height:	5 m (16 ft)
Weight:	Up to 3,600 kg (8,000 lb)
Diet:	Probably herbivorous

A male Gigantoraptor stamps his feet and shakes his brightly coloured neck plumes as he tries to impress a female.

The three young Oviraptors were found in the Gobi Desert, in Mongolia, in 2017. Since then, several other similar fossil groups have been found.

Snuggling siblings

The fossilised remains of three Oviraptor youngsters were found huddled together. They were all the same age and probably siblings or cousins snuggling up together when they died. This suggests that some dinosaurs, like many birds, roosted together in groups for warmth and company.

NESTING SITES

Some dinosaurs bred in colonies like modern birds. The remains of several nesting sites have been found, including a well-preserved Therizinosaurus colony in the Gobi Desert, in Mongolia, with 17 clutches containing more than 50 eggs. Scientists think that the dinosaurs clustered together for company, but also as protection from hungry predators tempted by their tasty big eggs.

Therizinosaurus

Lived:	Mongolia, 85–70 MYA
Length:	Up to 10 m (33 ft)
Weight:	Up to 6,000 kg (13,200 lb)
Diet:	Uncertain; probably mainly herbivorous

Therizinosaurus

These large, odd-looking theropods lived in Mongolia during the Late Cretaceous. First discovered in 1948, their fossils were originally believed to be from huge, turtle-like reptiles. More recent discoveries have shown they had feathers and probably looked like giant, bizarre birds.

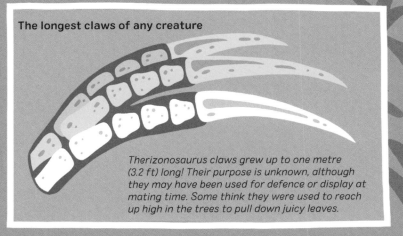

The longest claws of any creature

Therizonosaurus claws grew up to one metre (3.2 ft) long! Their purpose is unknown, although they may have been used for defence or display at mating time. Some think they were used to reach up high in the trees to pull down juicy leaves.

Therizonosaurus mothers were too big and heavy to sit on their eggs; they would have crushed them. They laid their round eggs in nests and probably covered them with sand or vegetation to keep them safe and warm until they hatched.

Together, the adult dinosaurs in the colony could defend their nests and young round the clock from ravenous predatory reptiles.

EGGS AND BABIES

Dinosaur babies hatched from eggs laid by adult females. Quite a few eggs have been found and we know that they were generally laid in groups, or clutches. Despite the fact that some dinosaurs were very large, their eggs were not much bigger than those of a modern ostrich. The baby dinosaurs grew very quickly after they hatched.

Embryos

A few fossilised eggs have been found with tiny embryos inside. Here you can see a baby Therizonosaurus inside its egg, with its long claws already quite well developed.

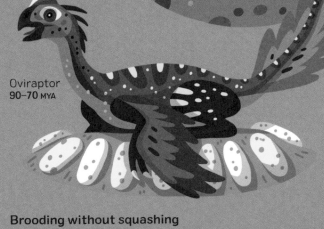

Oviraptor
90–70 MYA

Brooding without squashing

Some large dinosaurs brooded their eggs by laying them around the outside of the nest. When they sat in the centre of the nest the eggs were protected and warmed by their mother's feathers without being crushed.

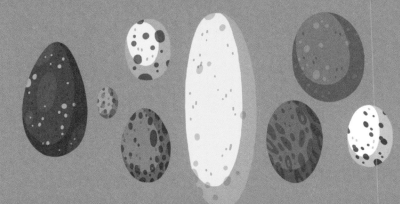

Colourful eggs

Dinosaur eggs were beautifully coloured and probably speckled like modern birds' eggs. They were oval or round and some were decorated with nodes and ridges.

AFRICA

Africa has a rich fossil record and a range of dinosaur remains have been found. Many early dinosaurs from the Triassic and early Jurassic are known, including Nyasasaurus, believed to be the earliest dinosaur ever discovered. Africa is also home to the largest predatory dinosaur in the world: Spinosaurus lived in modern-day North Africa towards the end of the dinosaur age.

Continents Adrift

LATE TRIASSIC

PANGAEA

LATE JURASSIC

LAURASIA

GONDWANA

LATE CRETACEOUS

LAURASIA

GONDWANA

The orange areas on the maps show what is now Africa. During the Triassic and Jurassic it was joined to South America and the two continents have many dinosaurs in common.

The oldest stegosaur

Stegosaurs were common across the northern landmass of Laurasia but far fewer have been found in southern Gondwana. Palaeontologists were happy to describe an entirely new species of stegosaur in 2019. Called *Ardratiklit boulahfa*, or mountain lizard, it was found in the Atlas Mountains in Morocco. It is the only stegosaur discovered in Africa, and the earliest stegosaur ever found.

Ouranosaurus

Ouranosaurus was a large duck-billed dinosaur that lived in Niger during the early Cretaceous. It had spines down its back that may have supported a sail for regulating its body temperature or for display, like Spinosaurus. Alternatively, the spines may have held a hump full of fat, like a modern camel. The fat would have been used for energy if no food was available.

Aardonyx
201–191 MYA

Aardonyx was a very early type of sauropod from South Africa. It usually stood on two legs, only occasionally dropping down onto all fours.

Ouranosaurus
125–94 MYA

Nyasasaurus is the oldest dinosaur ever found. Its discovery pushed the dawn of the age of dinosaurs back by 10 to 15 million years.

Massospondylus
200–183 MYA

Nyasasaurus
247–240 NYA

Mother takes care

Scientists were excited when they found the fossilised remains of an early Jurassic dinosaur nesting site in South Africa. Several clutches of Massospondylus eggs were found and providing more evidence that dinosaurs nested in colonies, like birds. These are the oldest dinosaur eggs ever discovered.

DINORAMA – KNOW IT ALL!
Top 10 African Dinosaur Facts & Records

1. WORLD'S LARGEST CARNIVOROUS DINOSAUR
Spinosaurus. It was taller and longer than T-Rex, but lighter.

2. EARLIEST KNOWN DINOSAUR IN THE WORLD
Nyasasaurus. About the size of a labrador, it lived in Tanzania.

3. WORLD'S OLDEST KNOWN DINOSAUR EGGS
Massospondylus eggs with embryos inside found in South Africa, dating to 190 million years ago.

4. ONE OF THE FIRST JURASSIC GIANTS
Ledumahadi. Found in South Africa in 2018.

5. RICHEST DINOSAUR FOSSIL SITE IN AFRICA
Tendaguru Hill in Tanzania.

6. GIANT EARLY RELATIVE OF THE MODERN CROCODILE
Sarcosuchus. It grew up to 9.6 metres (31 ft) long and was covered head to tail with osteoderms (bony scales).

7. LARGEST AFRICAN DINOSAUR
Giraffatitan. It was about twice as tall as a giraffe. It is one of the largest animals ever to have lived on land.

8. DINOSAUR WHOSE NAME MEANS "CROCODILE MIMIC"
Suchomimus. It had 120 teeth in its long snout, perfect for catching fish.

9. MESOZOIC ANIMALS THAT ARE STILL ALIVE TODAY
Coelacanth fish. Relatives of the huge Mawsonia still cruise the deeps of the Indian Ocean.

10. DINOSAUR CANNIBAL
Majungasaurus. One of the few known dinosaurs to prey on its own species.

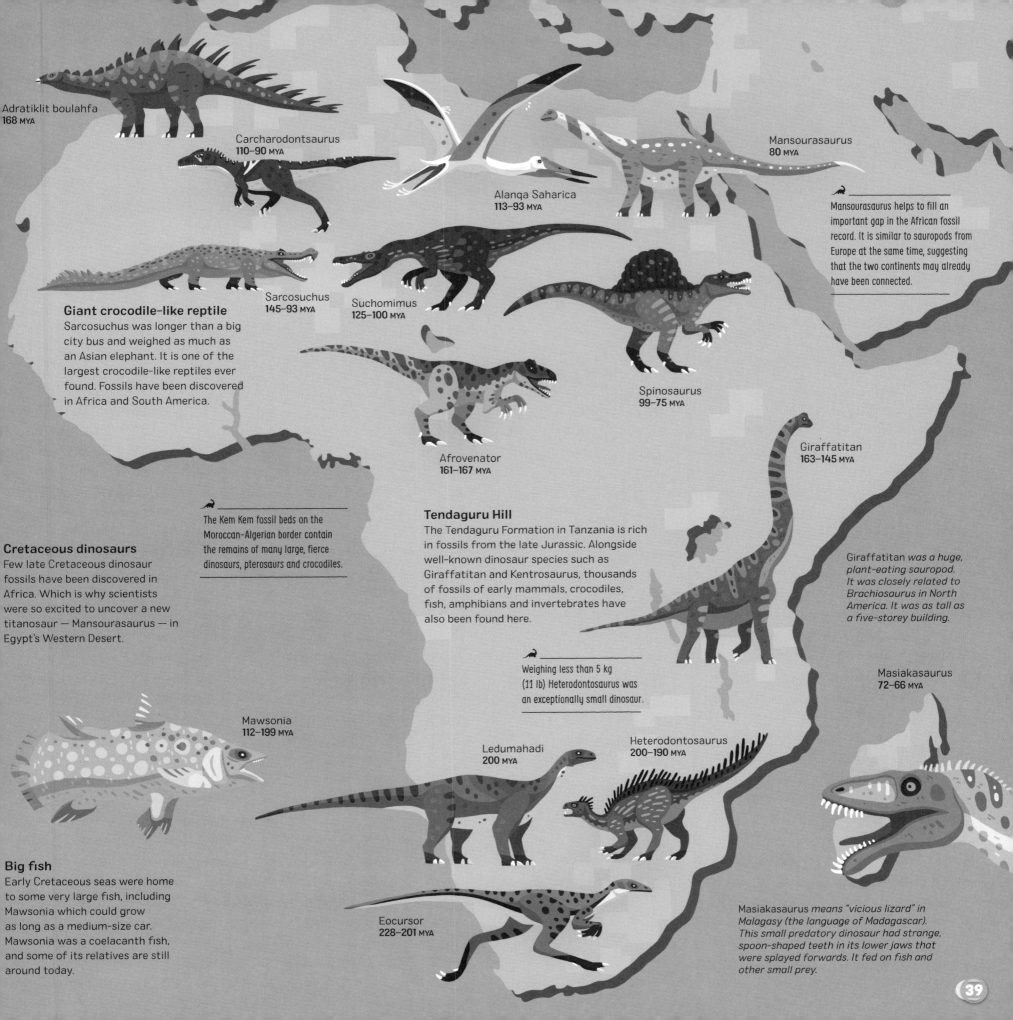

Adratiklit boulahfa
168 MYA

Carcharodontsaurus
110–90 MYA

Alanqa Saharica
113–93 MYA

Mansourasaurus
80 MYA

Mansourasaurus helps to fill an important gap in the African fossil record. It is similar to sauropods from Europe at the same time, suggesting that the two continents may already have been connected.

Sarcosuchus
145–93 MYA

Suchomimus
125–100 MYA

Giant crocodile-like reptile
Sarcosuchus was longer than a big city bus and weighed as much as an Asian elephant. It is one of the largest crocodile-like reptiles ever found. Fossils have been discovered in Africa and South America.

Spinosaurus
99–75 MYA

Giraffatitan
163–145 MYA

Afrovenator
161–167 MYA

Cretaceous dinosaurs
Few late Cretaceous dinosaur fossils have been discovered in Africa. Which is why scientists were so excited to uncover a new titanosaur — Mansourasaurus — in Egypt's Western Desert.

The Kem Kem fossil beds on the Moroccan-Algerian border contain the remains of many large, fierce dinosaurs, pterosaurs and crocodiles.

Tendaguru Hill
The Tendaguru Formation in Tanzania is rich in fossils from the late Jurassic. Alongside well-known dinosaur species such as Giraffatitan and Kentrosaurus, thousands of fossils of early mammals, crocodiles, fish, amphibians and invertebrates have also been found here.

Giraffatitan was a huge, plant-eating sauropod. It was closely related to Brachiosaurus in North America. It was as tall as a five-storey building.

Masiakasaurus
72–66 MYA

Weighing less than 5 kg (11 lb) Heterodontosaurus was an exceptionally small dinosaur.

Mawsonia
112–199 MYA

Ledumahadi
200 MYA

Heterodontosaurus
200–190 MYA

Big fish
Early Cretaceous seas were home to some very large fish, including Mawsonia which could grow as long as a medium-size car. Mawsonia was a coelacanth fish, and some of its relatives are still around today.

Eocursor
228–201 MYA

Masiakasaurus means "vicious lizard" in Malagasy (the language of Madagascar). This small predatory dinosaur had strange, spoon-shaped teeth in its lower jaws that were splayed forwards. It fed on fish and other small prey.

FEARSOME FISHERS

The largest of all the carnivorous dinosaurs, Spinosaurus roamed the marshlands and waterways that covered much of North Africa in the Cretaceous. Equally at home on land or in the water, this giant predator hunted the large fish that lived in the shallows. Standing knee-deep in the water, completely still, it used its keen eyesight to find the darting fish, waiting to strike at just the right moment with its fearsome teeth and claws.

The jaws of the sawfish were elongated and lined with teeth that stuck out bizarrely to the sides. The teeth had backward facing barbs, like harpoons. The sawfish probably used them for defence, slashing at predators. They also had small, normal teeth inside their mouths for chewing.

The riddle of the sail
Scientists have puzzled about the purpose of Spinosaurus' sail ever since it was discovered. Some think it was for display, to attract a partner at mating time. Others believe it was used to regulate body temperature, or to store fat for energy when food was scarce.

The sail stood between 1.5–2 metres (5–6 ft) tall and was supported by long neural spines covered in skin. Spinosaurus fossils have been found in Egypt and Morocco.

Spinosaurus

Lived:	North Africa, 99–75 MYA
Length:	Up to 18 m (59 ft)
Weight:	Up to 7,500 kg (15,500 lb)
Diet:	Carnivorous (fish, meat)

Spinosaurus *was a strong swimmer, paddling with its back legs and also using its tail to propel itself along.*

Giant sawfishes' jaws were lined with teeth

The sawfishes were also feared predators. Their eyes were positioned on the tops of their skulls so they could spot prey. Their teeth were barbed to stop prey escaping.

The giant sawfishes *grew up to three times as long as a tall man.*

Spinosaurus had elongated jaws more like those of a modern crocodile than most other dinosaurs.

Onchopristis - Giant Sawfish

Lived:	North Africa 95–66 MYA
Length:	Up to 8 m (26 ft)
Weight:	Up to 900 kg (2,000 lb)
Diet:	Piscivore (fish)

MADAGASCAR - A WORLD APART

Today the island of Madagascar lies off the coast of Africa but during most of the Mesozoic it was connected to India. Fossils are quite different from those in Africa, and the dinosaurs excavated here have more in common with those from India. There are also some unique species that have only been discovered on the island.

Beelzebufo
70–66 MYA

Beelzebufo, or the "devil frog," was the largest frog that ever lived. The size of a large beach ball, it was very aggressive and would gobble up prey with its outsize mouth.

Rahonavis
72–66 MYA

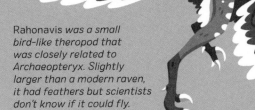

Rahonavis was a small bird-like theropod that was closely related to Archaeopteryx. Slightly larger than a modern raven, it had feathers but scientists don't know if it could fly.

Many of the dinosaurs found in Madagascar come from the late Cretaceous Maevarano Formation in the northeast. The light sandstone there has preserved the fossils very well and many complete skeletons have been found in excellent condition.

Majungasaurus
72–66 MYA

Majungasaurus was a large predatory dinosaur that lived in Madagascar during the late Cretaceous. It is one of the few dinosaurs known to have preyed on members of its own species.

AUSTRALASIA & ANTARCTICA

Antarctica has no permanent inhabitants. Scientists go there for a few months at a time, usually in the summer, and return home again to analyse their finds.

Fewer dinosaur fossils have been found in Australasia and Antarctica than elsewhere. This is not because dinosaurs didn't live there, but rather that both continents are vast and sparsely populated with extreme climates and these conditions make fossil hunting challenging. In the last two decades there has been a sharp increase in dinosaur finds on both continents driven by new technology and unflagging interest in dinosaurs.

Discovering Antarctic dinosaurs

The first Antarctic dinosaur fossil was not discovered until 1986. It was an ankylosaur called Antarctopelta (see below). Since then a number of different species have been found, especially in the Transantarctic Mountains that run across the continent.

Continents Adrift

LATE TRIASSIC

P A N G A E A

LATE JURASSIC

L A U R A S I A

G O N D W A N A

LATE CRETACEOUS

L A U R A S I A

G O N D W A N A

The orange areas show Australia and Antarctica. They were part of the same landmass for most of the dinosaur age, only splitting apart during the last part of the Cretaceous.

Cryolophosaurus
199–183 MYA

Cryolophosaurus was the first meat-eating dinosaur found in Antarctica. It was also the largest carnivore in the region and one of the biggest predators of its time. It had an unusual fan-shaped crest on its head.

Morrosaurus
70–66 MYA

Morrosaurus was an iguanodont.

The Antarctanax was a fairly small archosaur, and an early ancestor of crocodiles and dinosaurs.

Trinisaura was a small, beaked, ornithopod dinosaur.

Trinisaura
83–70 MYA

TRANSANTARCTIC MOUNTAINS

South Pole

Antarctopelta
83–72 MYA

Antarctanax
About 250 MYA

Glacialisaurus
199–182 MYA

Australian dinosaurs

The first Australian dinosaur fossil was found in Victoria in 1903. Since then another two dozen or so species have been described. Most dinosaurs have been found in the eastern half of Australia, but a few have also come to light in western Australia.

Over 20 different species of dinosaurs have left tracks in the 130-million-year-old sandstone at Broome, Western Australia.

Broome

Yangtzepus tracks About 130 MYA

Kunbarrasaurus
119–113 MYA

"Banjo" Australovenator
About 95 MYA

Wintonotitan
100–94 MYA

Rich fossil locations
The Winton Formation in Queensland is one of the richest dinosaur fossil areas. Some of the fossils at Lightning Ridge in New South Wales are made of opal (a beautiful gemstone).

**Ozraptor
About 170 MYA**

Diamantinasaurus
100–90 MYA

WINTON FORMATION

Dating from the mid-Jurassic, Ozraptor is the earliest known Australian dinosaur.

Australovenator
99–93 MYA

● **Lightning Ridge**

Leaellynasaura
122–109 MYA

Rhoetosaurus was a large Jurassic sauropod. It walked on tip toes, much as elephants do today.

Rhoetosaurus
170–168 MYA

DINORAMA – KNOW IT ALL!
Top 10 Australasia & Antarctica Dinosaur Facts & Records

1. WORLD'S RICHEST DINOSAUR TRACKS SITE
Broome, Western Australia. Tracks of at least 21 different species have been found there.

2. MOST COMPLETE PTEROSAUR EVER FOUND IN AUSTRALIA
Iron Dragon. It had more than 100 teeth in its small jaws.

3. FIRST CARNIVOROUS DINOSAUR FOUND IN ANTARCTICA
Cryolophosaurus. Its name means "frozen crested lizard."

4. FIRST DINOSAUR FOSSIL DISCOVERED IN ANTARCTICA
Antarcticopelta. This herbivorous dinosaur had thick body armour

and many spikes. We don't know if it had a club on its tail.

5. DINOSAUR FOSSILS MADE OF OPAL
Rare and beautiful, they come from Lightning Ridge in NSW, Australia.

6. A NEW ZEALAND REPTILE THAT LIVED ALONGSIDE THE DINOSAURS
Tuatara. They are still alive. Tuatara look like big lizards and can live to 100.

7. ONE OF THE WORLD'S BIGGEST PLESIOSAURS
The Elasmosaur recently found in Antarctica.

8. A LATE CRETACEOUS ANTARCTIC BIRD
Vegavis. We don't know if it survived the cataclysm that wiped out the dinosaurs.

9. TITANOSAUR THAT HIKED FROM SOUTH AMERICA, ACROSS ANTARCTICA TO AUSTRALIA
Savannasaurus.

10. EARLIEST KNOWN AUSTRALIAN DINOSAUR
Ozraptor. The name means "Australian thief."

Muttaburrasaurus
105–93 MYA

Tuatara
From 250 MYA

The New Zealand Tuatara is the only surviving member of a family of reptiles that lived alongside the dinosaurs. They first appeared 250 million years ago, and are sometimes referred to as "living dinosaurs."

Taniwhasaurus
86–66 MYA

Fossils of the Taniwhasaurus mosasaur were first found in New Zealand. It is named after the Taniwha, or "water monsters" in Maori legends. It grew up to 12 metres (39 ft) long.

**Iron dragon
About 96 MYA**

LIVING IN ANTARCTICA

Antarctica is now buried under an ice sheet a mile deep, but during the Cretaceous it was covered in swampy, temperate rainforest. It was warmer than it is now, but still a long way south. In winter, the sun didn't rise above the horizon for months at a time. Despite the long dark winters, a wide range of dinosaurs lived here.

Scientists were amazed when they found fossils of rainforest in Antarctica. The plants and animals that lived there would have needed special adaptations to survive the long months of winter darkness.

Elasmosaur
About 70 MYA

Savannasaurus *was a titanosaur that came from South America. Fossils have been found in Australia so it seems that the ancestors of these huge creatures walked from South America across Antarctica to Australia about 100 million years ago, before Australia drifted north.*

Diluvicursor
115–110 MYA

Savannasaurus
105–95 MYA

Vegavis
68–66 MYA

Late Cretaceous birds
Footprints and fossils of Cretaceous birds have been found in the Antarctic. The earliest penguins may also have evolved at this time. The fish-eating Vegavis shown here lived in the seas alongside the giant elasmosaur. It was related to modern ducks, and fossils of its vocal chords suggest that it honked like a goose.

Azhdarchid pterosaur
70 MYA

This large Antarctic pterosaur is known from a single fossil. Scientists think it had a wingspan of almost 5 metres (16 ft).

The giant elasmosaur found in Antarctica dates from just before the mass extinction event that wiped out most other animals around 66 million years ago.

Galleonosaurus was a small ornithopod dinosaur that lived in Australia and Antarctica in the early Cretaceous.

Galleonosaurus
About 125 MYA

Antarctopelta
83–70 MYA

Sea monsters

Scientists recently discovered the fossilised skeleton of a giant elasmosaur in Antarctica. The huge creature may have weighed as much as 13,500 kg (30,000 lb) and been 12 metres (40 ft) long. This is one of the largest plesiosaurs ever found, and it shows that the Antarctic seas must have been teeming with life to provide food for such a large animal.

THE END OF THE DINOSAURS

The Mesozoic era ended about 66 million years ago with a mass extinction. Most scientists believe that a huge asteroid smashed into our planet, wiping out about three quarters of all life. Almost all the dinosaurs died out, leaving just a few species that are the ancestors of modern birds.

Impact!

The asteroid measured about 10 km (6 mi) across and the impact released as much energy as millions of nuclear bombs exploding all at once. It triggered devastating tsunamis at sea and wildfires on land. The dust and debris hurled into the air blocked out the Sun for years. Starved of light, plants could not carry out photosynthesis and died out. Many of the animals that survived the initial impact became extinct because they had nothing to eat.

Enantiornithes *were very like modern birds, except that most species had teeth. No modern birds have teeth.*

WHO SURVIVED?

Only a few ground-dwelling species survived the asteroid strike. Even the most common birds, a group called the Enantiornithes, all died out. They lived in trees and when the forests were destroyed their habitat disappeared.

How do we know?

The asteroid theory was first proposed by father-and-son scientists Luis and Walter Alvarez in 1980. They found a high level of a metal called iridium in the geological record exactly when the dinosaurs went extinct. Iridium is rare in the Earth's crust, but is plentiful in asteroids. Later, scientists found a huge impact crater left by an asteroid strike on the coast of the Yucatan Peninsula, in Mexico.

Alternative theories

Not all scientists are convinced by the asteroid theory. Some think that extreme volcanic activity over many years had filled the skies with carbon dioxide and other gases, cooling the planet and causing the slow decline of the dinosaurs. In this scenario, the asteroid strike was just the last straw.

The Deccan Traps

Towards the end of the Cretaceous period, there were volcanic eruptions over a vast area of northern India that lasted for about 30,000 years. Lava covered the land and gas and debris darkened the skies. This may have led to the decline of many forms of life on Earth.

INDEX